Visions

Prophecies & Revelations

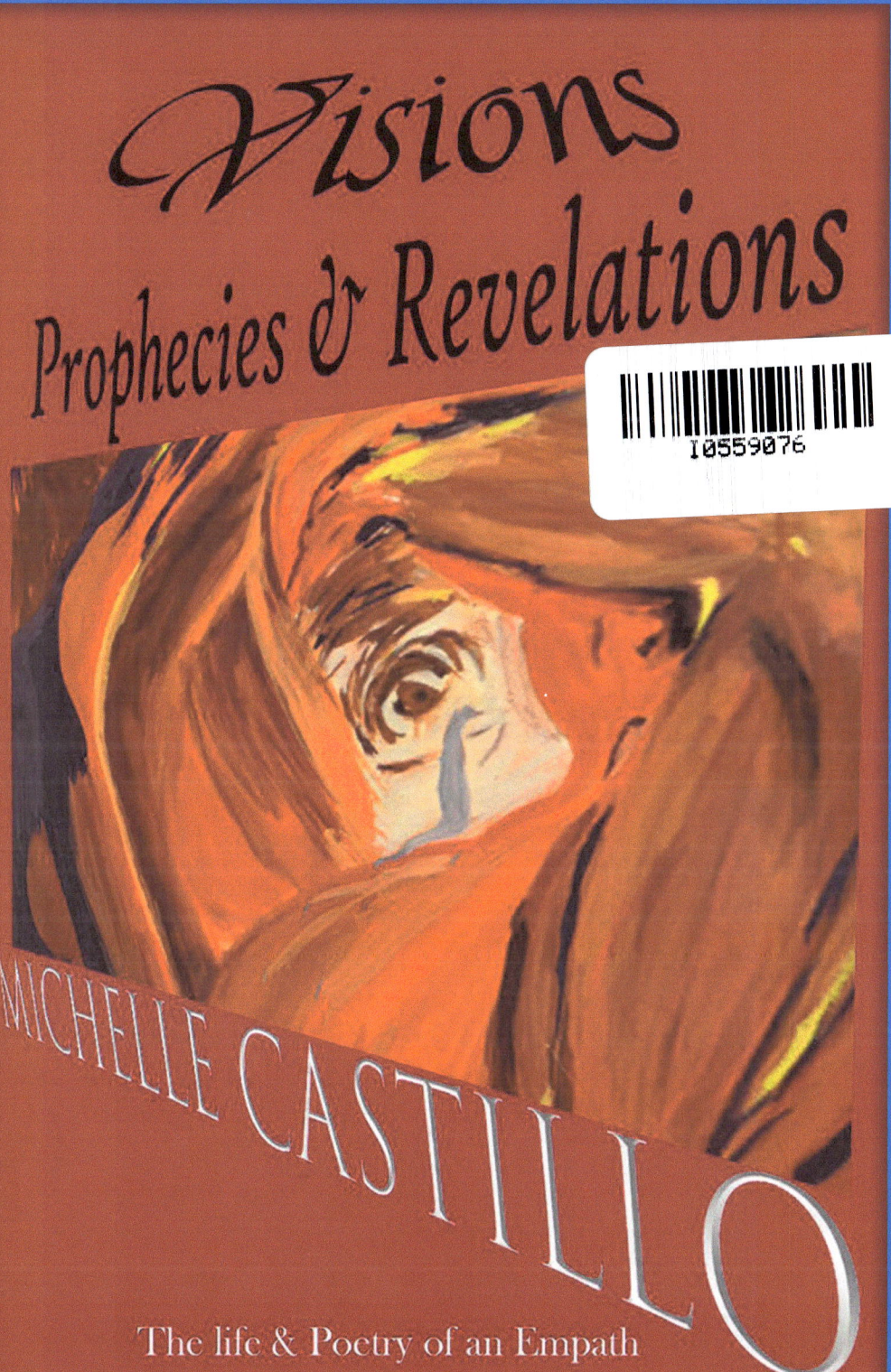

MICHELLE CASTILLO

The life & Poetry of an Empath

Table of Contents

I find the clouds of Albuquerque beautiful and have quite a collection.

One bright Sunday afternoon after church, I stopped at a gas station on Unser in Albuquerque, New Mexico; as usual, I looked up, turned around, and there in the sky was a beautiful cloud in the shape of a heart. If one has to have a cloud over their head, let it be the heart of God.

KNOWING YOU

Through the love that kept me blind,
  I'm so grateful you came in time.
Life became a maze, and I knew not
  where to turn
  When I saw you, I felt the pain, and my
heart began to burn.
  Through the dark, I wandered lonely,
seeking you in my body only.
  Though the love that was so blind, your
Love reached out and touched my mind.
  Something has grown that is so sweet,
through all my trials, for now, we meet.
  At first, I knew what you were, but like
The the fog you were not there.
  You stood before me in the form of man,
and I reached out to touch your hand.
  It learned that very day, desire for man was
 not the way.
  Through your loving eyes, I see how much
you love me.
  When you showed me how much you cared,
My heart I opened, my heart I shared.
  I felt such trembling from seeing you, and
felt such joy in knowing what you can do.
  Life has new meaning from deep within,
and now I can say we are more than friends.
  My most profound thought is with you I share,
because in my heart, I know you care.
  Let me share this love so new because
I am happiest when I'm with you.

OBEDIENCE IN YOUR LOVE

The people have gone astray,
  They've forgotten your laws.
They've forgotten your ways.
    Where is the youth of America?
Their thoughts have gone astray.
    Everywhere I see hatred, foulness,
the prejudice that never seems
to die, my eyes they see, my ears
 they hear my voice it cries.
  For America has gone astray,
for the youth, I pray, and all those
 dead insides.
 I need your Help, my Lord; in
 the face of adversity, your word
 is enough.
    The light of your love, I want to
share that lifts the darkness from
    those who do not care.
Their minds completely stolen
 from our God above.
Their hearts are hardened and
    unfulfilled with His Love.

TRUTH

HE DWELLS IN ME IN THE SPIRIT OF
MY SOUL
  THROUGH HIS EYES, I SEE THE
BEAUTY OF THINGS APPEAR BEFORE ME.
   AND THROUGH HIS HEART I FEEL
 FOR THE THINGS WHICH FADES AWAY.
  MY LOVE FOR YOU IS SO STRONG,
I GIVE TO YOU AT WILL.
  YOUR LOVE LETS ME SEE THE LIFE
BEFORE ME UNFOLD.
  I SEE THE LIES AND DECEIT FOR
 THOSE WHO NEED YOU.
  I WANT SO MUCH TO REACH OUT
 MY HAND TO WARM THEIR COLD
COLD HEARTS.
  TO BRING THEM INTO THE LIGHT OF LOVE.
 BY YOUR WILL THEY WILL COME
  TO KNOW YOU.
I HAVE ONLY TO SHOW LOVE, OH, LORD!
  REACH FORTH YOUR HAND AND TOUCH
THE HEARTS OF THE LOST.
  I LOVE WHEN I LAY IN YOUR PRESENCE
AND DWELL ON YOUR BEAUTY.
  YOU ARE TRULY A DIVINE MATRIX.

....

"When you get your most brilliant ideas, did you ever stop
to think that it was the Lord who did that.?
   And when you wrote your most inspiring poetry on that
sunny afternoon feeling so beautiful and peaceful, did
you ever stop to think that it was the Lord who did that?
And when your friends love you for your quick wit, and fantastic
sense of humor, and just being you, did you
ever stop to think? And when you did stop to think, did
you thank God?

Photography Michelle Castillo   Albuquerque-2010

The Essence of Being

To joy, to joy,
May it be discovered
May it never be hidden.

To life to life,
May it be discovered
May it be enjoyed.

To Love to love,
May it be discovered
And may it always bring
joy to your life.

Painting by *Michelle Castillo*

Living in Fullness Everlasting

I have much to learn from you,
  your wisdom is so hidden.
Yet, day by day, I see your knowledge,
  revealed in such a way to make
my life is so true.
  Your love is all I need
to find my way ahead, to walk
  completely in fulfillment, to
understand all you've said.
  When you genuinely love me,
when you genuinely understand, only
  then will you know me, and
love with your heart again. Then
  only together we will be as one in
the light once more, then hand
  in hand, we will walk, through
only open doors.
For together in love, can we
  have a love for others to see.

And spread that love around the
world and live-in harmony.
   Together we can overcome, the
hurt and the pain.
   You have only to look up, my love,
and feel the power of love again, and
   when you do, then start to
embrace it with your loving thoughts,
 embrace it with your heart,
embrace it with your inner being
   only then we'll never part.
When you have my love,
   then take the time to feel,
the warmth of love's embrace.
   When you have my love, only
   then you will see the glow
 about, then my love, will you
be in love, in love without
 a doubt.

Finding true Help

Life is hard, we give little, without
the key, we're caught in a storm
& Life becomes a riddle.
We must become aware
of where we tread, and what
was said.
For our word is our belief,
for the heart to find its destiny.
We must find our way from the
Crowd before the crowds
becomes a maze.
Beware of the constant confusion,
listen not to conversations of
mind boggling illusions.
Meditate, become whole with
your soul, unites to restore it to light.
Look up into oneness, your heart
you will see, so peaceful the ocean,
so calm is the sea.
Look not behind you, let your heart
not stray,
like trees in a storm, uncontrollably,
wickedly, violently it sways.
Don't do like the next person, why
travel their road? You were once
righteous, and now you need to be told.
You left a good road you were on at first,
now you are begging for food, and its
liquor you thirst?
You have a friend One that is true,
One that is willing to help you,
He'll pick you up when you are down,
Only He can turn your whole life around.

My painting of my son & photoshop S.F G.G Bridge

My Son Jason & grandson Julius

Forever my Joy

My love, such joy in watching
my son overcome his anxiety.
Conquering negative thoughts
so confidently.
I shall never forget the smile
that arose as he looked up at me
with a look that   glowed.
Wonderfully my love got through
to break apart, the darkness that
has shielded his eyes and hardened
his heart.
My love has shown him the
difference between light and dark,
and it didn'ttake long for him
to become confidently strong.
Unyielding to the temptations
of the mind.
How it can torture, confuse
and deceive him in time.
He draws to him all that is good,
Just like I knew he would.

PAINTING BY *MICHELLE CASTILLO* TITLE "*PTSD*" DEDICATED TO *WOMEN AGAINST DOMESTIC VIOLENCE*

TO BEHOLD LIFE BEFORE YOU, IS TO LIVE LIFE ANEW

HE HEARS MY CRIES

My Father in Heaven breathes
in me.
Once again, your breath of life.
For I am dead in life, and I have
lost My way.
Free me, father, from the
hell of torment.
Cleanse me, father, from
the mud of hate.
It is such a fine line for me
to conceive Your wonderment.
For it is with much hope that I
endure my life as minor cuts
and bruises.
Your love for me is so profound.
The simplest of suffering touches
you.
Feeling your compassion,
I can only ask, who Has the
unconquerable power to hold
back the rain?

2015 AngelMan   By Michelle Castillo

Wisdom

"I have in me the capabilities to bring forth the knowledge and Words I need to express myself without feeling inhibited about them.

If I wish to speak on a level in which only a few people understand I will do so, but they have yet to experience what is being explained.

They may grasp the simple terms, but still, they search Profoundly for its true meaning."

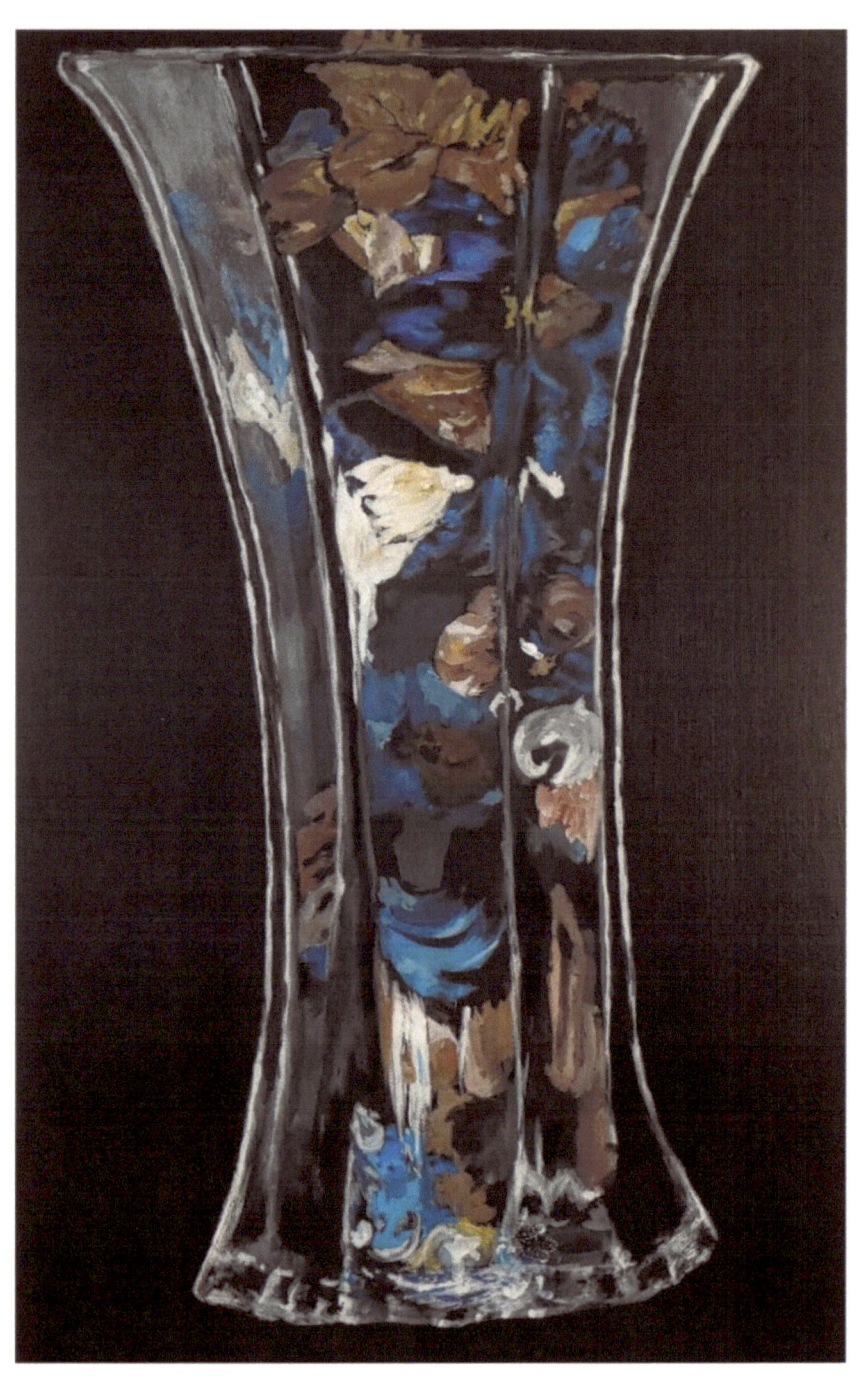

Painting by Michelle Castillo

14

God's Voice and his rose of remembrance

A poem I once wrote, my love, had so much joy, And feelings,
  It was for you, my love; did it send you reeling?
Once written for a mân I thought wase my friend.
 These feelings I've always had, my love, believing
 I had a friend once again.
 Am I meant to love you? to see you through your most
harrowing moments, to relieve your tensions and relieve your
 most trying thoughts, then.
The love I felt to make you, But I suffered
 from false truth.
I was born to be a woman; With God I grew to be a lady,
  I love you, my God. You are my Lord, and I am so
Proud to walk beside you, as you lovingly hold my hand.
 You treat me like a queen, my Lord, you're in my heart my love,
 You walk with me among the crowds, as you shin your
 light from above.
The world is full of changes, and the changes are bad enough.
 Let me not change with the world; let the world change
with us.
  As I strive to live Godly life; May I Love and give.
I dare not listen to those who say, "to the way
 of the world, we must live".
****

Painting by Michelle Castillo   UNM *2013*

LEGOS OF LIFE

*If we do not concentrate on our life, we will fall short of our
goals. We must improve our lifestyle daily in
order to continue the road to success. Life is complicated only
because we make it hard. We must find in ourselves the
power to concentrate, the knowledge to understand, and
The wisdom to remain true to our goals.*

*Life is a mystery, a puzzle, a building block. We must figure
out and find the pieces, then we begin to build. When a piece is
out of place, our whole structure falls apart, but when
there is someone there to help and put that piece back in
place and set you back on your path, then together you have
a strong foundation, and together you have life.*

THE VISION

It's harvest time, America!
The Lord has planted His seeds.
It's time to take root and grow,
for how else Can he meet your needs
only through his Laws can you know.
Right now, you feel the need, but the
Lord, You have not seen.
You will always wonder, and you will
Always Be grim because he is calling you
to acknowledge him.
Go to him; he's calling you to learn and to
Receive, don't turn your backs. Lookup
And believe!
It's harvest time, America, seeds
Have been Planted,
the Lord is showing you today that
He gave you many chances.
The time has come for awakening, and
the time is come for reaping!
Our children are suffering immorality
because the Lord's children are sleeping.
Everything in life has meaning; what the
Lord says and does is true. Let me
Prove it by sharing a piece of scripture
with you.
Good shepherds know precisely
to do.
When We start leading our children
in paths of righteousness.
As you can see what our sleeping
has cost.
Our children stand on corners
like sheep that are lost.
We need to awaken to the sound
of his trod,
then we will continue as one nation
Under God.
Let us get together with God who alone,
Blessed America, our home, sweet home!

17

The Attraction

A circle within a circle within a
 A circle is the only way I can describe it.
  How hard it is to penetrate enough
to get some feeling of your understanding
  I am susceptible to the shield you put
up before me.
  I want only to share with you as a friend,
but my quest for an open friendship just
  It cannot be, for we are much too profound,
and any act of profusion may severe any
  Contact we may have forged.
Your armor is strong, but your words are
  as for knives, they are not intentionally
thrown, but your message is sharp.
  You are untouchable and genuinely one
who with few words inspires deep
  inhibitions within me.
I am hurt, but I am not saddened; I cry,
  but I do not cry tears of anguish, only
tears of awareness that surfaced from
  So deep within me.
I sit in fear of wrong judgment of you, yet
  I do not need to judge, but only to see
through my heart, the good in you.
  You are indeed a beautiful person with
whom I have only the most profound
respect and highest regard for your
wellbeing.
Like a Rosebud so inspiritingly charged
 with the pulsating urge to reach beyond
the circle that keeps us from growing in
 everlasting Friendship.

Spiritual Veil

Yes, I am discovering the whole of me, the dark
  Hidden depths of me.
 Surfacing occasionally to grab reality,
  Yet, if he proves to be hurtful, again, I have
 only to submerge into a world and be hidden.
  Analysts are diver submerging, discovering,
 admiring the depths of wonder, knowing what is
  at hand, but not what lies below sea level.
They have reached the depths of my other world,
  A world in which no ordinary man on land can
 Decipher.
  I am the extension of your love and give you the
 Curiosity and depth perception to know the
  Mysteries of the deep.
In my peaceful Beauty will lure you, my storms will
 Inspire you.
I am the first discovery of the deep sea; I am not a
 diver, nor an analyst, but I know what it's like to be
submerged in a world where no one understands me.
  I know the peace, silence, love, and freedom it gives
to one who seeks it.
  The shore cannot understand the sea. The man
that is in the world, can but only understand the
  Shores. It is only in the world of depth and wonder
can one perceive and possess the mysteries of life
 both above and below in which only peace will
Obtain.

Abstract self-portrait   *2013*

Photoshop creation by Michelle Castillo

Abstract painting by Michelle Castillo

SOFT WHISPERS OF COMFORT

Do not cry, my child; time is running behind you.
Fear not the rain, for it falls before you.
Run not from the thunder, for it is lightning that strikes.
Feel free to dance a new dance to the
days that go by and are gone.
Feel brave, for your love is the barricade
against a cruel world.
Fear not the fire, my child, I am the big
oak tree and you, my love, are safe within.

PHOTOGRAPHY BY   MICHELLE CASTILLO   2018

Painting by Michelle Castillo   UNM 2013

The Comforter

I feel like a bird in a cage, unable to fly freely. I can only fly so far. I want to fly over the next horizon to explore new wonders.

I can only explore new wonders from what's hidden within my boundaries.

Here in my boundaries, I dwell and gather my wisdom.

Yet, once I have stepped over my boundaries, I am once again a pupil.

I sit in silence and listen to learn new things, and when you ask about this place, I speak with wisdom and knowledge.

· ·

"Give thought to what you are thinking, but don't get lost in your thoughts."

The Saying of "Lady Matrix #ladymatrixsayings

FROM WORDS TO COLOR

For all the beautiful people with words of Poem,
for those who like to stay at home and write
melodies in peace and alone.
For love in them are so inspired, for alone you
are not, together we tire.
Your vast feeling of wonders is from deep inside, to
project into colors and shapes for others to realize.
The world does not understand your beautiful views,
it's only those who understand and love you.
Write your poems "retain! Retain! Retain! so that
your words will survive and remain.
Many of you suffered for want of escape, that you
would project a message that would later become
great!
So sweet the imagination so deep is your
thoughts, for us to catch up, for others you fought.
goodness follows the one who suffered for Deity,
and Goodness suffers in this sinful society, and
sincerity derives from honesty.
Reaching out as an invitation to open up, inviting
the poor at heart to dine at your sup.
Catching feelings and emotions on canvas with each
stroke.
Alas! When finished, overwhelming and sweltering
tears do choke.
For the world will not be as you see, the beautiful
are you who suffer for their sanity?
The spiritual will realize from this bit of news,
that this world was never meant for one
as beautiful as you.

Painting by Michelle Castillo-   *Blood Moon Prophecy 2013*

2013 GON Photo by Michelle Castillo

Starry Night

Lord, I understand what you tried to say
to me, how you suffered for your sanity.
   Vincent Van Gough knew you, yet the
world would not listen; they did not
   know-how perhaps they'll listen now.
Morning fields of amber gray, John
   Lennon felt the same way.
No one would listen when he tried to
   explain, and through his quick wit
he brought them pain.
There's a pattern the follow the Lord
Jesus Christ and all good souls suffer
   your same strife
How you suffered for your sanity, and
how you tried to set them free.
The world did not listen; it didn't know
   how perhaps they'll listen now.
The recording artist carries all the means,
   why good men die like Martin Luther
King.
 For they could not love you even though
 your love is true,
I could have told you, Diana, this world
   was never meant for one as beautiful
as you.
   It's people who emulate you and try to
take a stand, only to find that the world
still does not understand,
   As the rich sit at home well at ease,
while your faithful struggle and die
   for world peace.
Stevie's Wonder melodies, his lyrics
   so calm is today's spiritual palms.
A palm is a song of Praise because you
   have been seen, not only by Wonder,
but also, by Green.

DEFYING GRAVITY

Photoshop work by Michelle Castillo

True Followers

Lord, I understand what you tried to say
  to me, how you suffered for your sanity.
Vincent Van Gough knew you, and like
  you they would not listen, they did not
know how, perhaps they'll listen now.
  Morning fields of amber, gray,
John Lennon felt the same way.
  How He suffered for His sanity, and how
He tried to set them free.
  The world did not listen, it does not know
how, perhaps they'll listen now.
  No one would listen when he tried to
explain, and through his quick wit he
  brought them pain.
There's a pattern that follows the Lord
  Jesus Christ, and all good souls suffer
his same strife.
  How He suffered for His sanity, and how
He tried to set them free.
  The world did not listen, it does not know
how, perhaps they'll listen now.
  The recording artist carries all the means,
why good men die like Martin Luther
  King.
For they could not love you though your
  love is true,
.I could have told you Diana, this world was
  never meant for one as beautiful as you.
It's people who emulate you Lord and try
  to take a stand, only to find that the
world still does not understand,
  As the rich sit at home well at ease,
while your faithful struggle and die
  for world peace.
Stevie's words, melodies, his lyrics
  so calm, soothing like a spiritual palm.
A palm a song of Praise because you
  have been seen, not only by Wonder
but also, by Green.

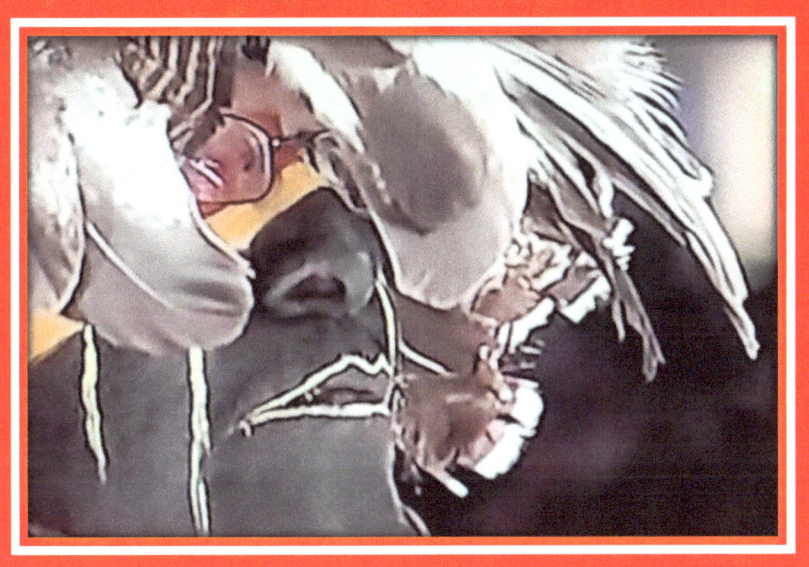

Photography by Michelle

SUBLIMITY

What is it I feel so deep inside? That
  brings me to my knees till I cry.
Could it be this world that troubles
 me deep inside?
Why is the world this way? as we
  struggle from day-to-day.
The loneliness of my room, the echoing
  sound of my cries
Looking at the world with tears in
  my eyes.
All the realization from internally to
  externally it spills.
To bring sight to the hidden things that
  silently kill.
Those are the little things that cause
  the greatest pain.
Reaching forth our hand in hopes that
  others will do the same.
Are we so busy with the day-to-day quest?
  we have only hateful and hurtful words
to express?
  You can speak life or death with a single
word, then to compliment, appreciate,
  words not heard.
 Let it be the beginning of the awareness
  Of God.
His Divine guidance that others find odd.
  If you feel you need no others love,
just remember you are truly loved from
  above.
The world! The World! So many just don't
  believe.
For the spiritual, the end doesn't always
  justified the means.

This Painting I did is of the unfinished Shirt on the dress form in the back. My brother was one of many living in a home with others infected with HIV, and he was chosen to do an interview with channel 5. My brother passed away in 1994, and he appointed me his power of attorney, and I arranged the memorial for him.

The painting is my dedication to him and his creative talent as a designer, & modern jazz dancer who worked with me a gymnast at the time to put together our talents to create a wonderful performance of dance.

RIP to my brother Donald Dean Castillo AKA Jazzy, and to all my brothers who have left This world.

Don Castillo

San Francisco, CA

35

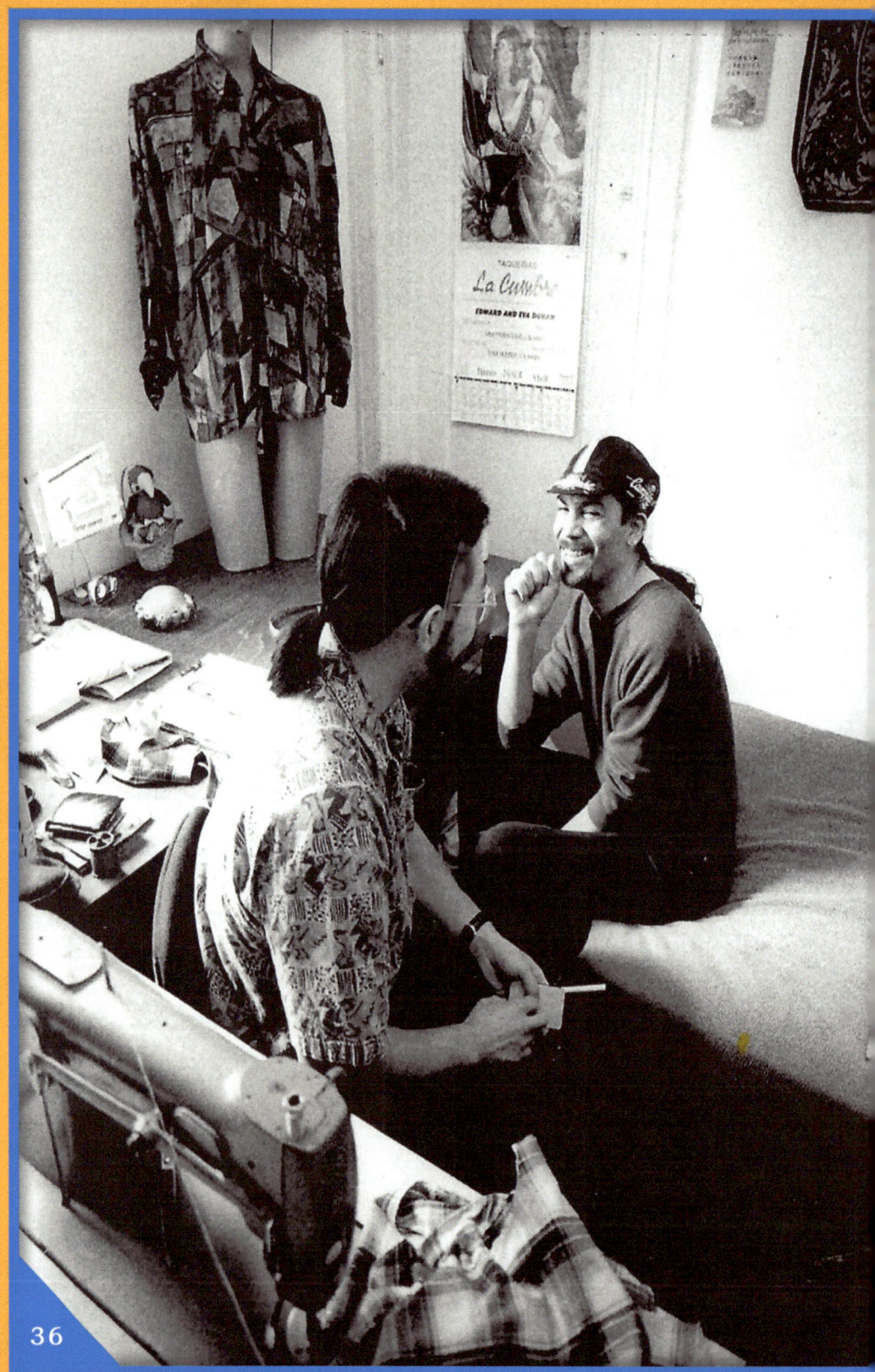

June 10 1971

CALIFORNIA DEBUT – Don Castillo and Angelina Cosca were featured in June 6 performance in San Francisco's Harding Theater of world premiere of "Interim," dance theater piece presented by Stanze Peterson troupe. Company has moved from New York to San Francisco.

"My thanks to all who supported me in my creativities.

My book is also dedicated to my talented family members & friends past & present."

www.ingramcontent.com/pod-product-compliance
Lightning Source LLC
Chambersburg PA
CBHW040849120626
46547CB00001B/91